MW01514383

clay POTS
TM
by M. Pié

Evergreen
PRESS

Clay Pots by Mark Pié

ISBN 1-58169-207-2
For Worldwide Distribution
Printed in the U.S.A.

Evergreen Press
P.O. Box 191540
Mobile, AL 36619

Introduction

We are the children of God. However, each of us shares a common, inescapable mortality. Whether ancient day patriarch or modern day pew polisher, at our best, we are mere earthen vessels; slightly cracked clay pots on the same shelf of life. I believe, sometimes that can be funny.

Clay Pots is an off-beat cartoon series that looks at Bible characters and situations with a little (O.K., a lot of) creative license. The cartoons were not created with the intent to belittle or disrespect anyone. But rather, to look past those "stained glass" images of flesh and blood mortals, who were "saved by grace" just like you and I were, and include them in on the fun. Life is often hard and sad. We should never be so spiritual as to miss the occasional respites of unexpected laughter God sends our way.

So, lighten up, Church! And, laugh a little more. After all, aren't we all clay pots?

Dedication

I want to dedicate this book to my wife Karen.
For 30 years she's been telling me to put my cartoons in a book.
And for 30 years, I've been coming up with one excuse after another
why I shouldn't. None of which were good reasons, I might add.
Well, I guess I've either run out of excuses or I finally saw
that she was right. I have a gift and maybe some folks
out there just might enjoy being
blessed by it.

So let's see if folks out there
are ready for my weirdness. This first one is
dedicated to you, babe. Let's pray that
it won't take me 30 more years
to produce the sequel.

LET THERE
BE LAUGHTER

BRINGING REAL MEANING TO THE PHRASE... WHO COULD THAT BE?
...AND IT WAS EVENING AND MORNING THE 4TH DAY.
RING! RING!
MPIE

ADAM GAVE NAMES TO ALL THE ANIMALS.
REPUBLICAN!

AFTER AWHILE, ADAM JUST COULDN'T COME UP WITH ANY NEW NAMES
I DUH KNOW. DAVE, GEORGE... UH... LEFTY

THE BABOON TOOK OFFENSE TO THE NAME ADAM GAVE HIM.
POW
MPLE

BEFORE EVE CAME ALONG, ADAM'S PROMS WERE A REAL DRAG.
MOONLIGHT OVER PARADISE

THINGS THAT WOULD HAVE BEEN GOOD TO HAVE AT THE MOMENT
ELECTRIC APPLES
EWW
MPIE

ADAM
AND
EVE'S
DOG
(AFTER THE FALL)

ADAM MADE SOME SHAMEFUL ATTEMPTS TO GET BACK IN THE GARDEN
PIZZA DELIVERY
GARDEN OF EDEN
MPIÉ

SOMETHING YOU SHOULD NEVER SAY TO AN ANGEL HOLDING A FLAMING SWORD
NICE DRESS.
MPIÉ

SOMEHOW CAIN KNEW HIS OFFERING WAS UNACCEPTABLE.
ALPIÉ

CONFUSION MANIFESTED ITSELF IN MANY WAYS AT THE TOWER OF BABEL PROJECT.

WHAT IF THE TOWER OF BABEL WAS COMPLETED?
ANYONE KNOW HOW WE GET DOWN?
MPÉ

ENOCH'S HIDE 'N SEEK RECORD IS UNBROKEN TO THIS DAY
?
?
MPIE

NECESSITY IS THE MOTHER OF INVENTION
A METHUSALAH BIRTHDAY CANDLE BLOWER

TWO PEOPLE NEVER SEEM TO CALL IT QUITS. METHUSALAH AND HIS FRIEND.
YO! METHUZ.
ROCKY
ROCKY

PATRIARCH COMMERCIAL
HELLO FRIENDS. METHUSALAH HERE, TELLING YOU THAT WITH PATRIARCH INSURANCE, THERE IS NO CHANCE OF CANCELATION NO MATTER HOW OLD YOU GET. HEE HEE HEE.
WPIE

ARK HUMOR
(ARK! ARK!)

NOAH'S PARANOID PET
aaawk! LOOKS LIKE RAIN. BETTER HURRY.

THINGS THAT WOULD HAVE BEEN GOOD TO HAVE AT THE MOMENT
INFLATABLE ARKS
HOW TO USE
THIS SIDE UP

NOAH'S DOG LOVED TO PLAY "FETCH THE PLUG"

NOAH WAS SURE HE HAD TWO DOGS WHEN HE BEGAN
DOGS
GATORS

NOAH KILLING TIME

FROM THE BEGINNING, EVERY FAMILY TRIP HAS BEEN THE SAME.
ARE WE THERE YET?
"I SPY SOMETHING... BLUE."
MPIE

AND THE DOVE RETURNED TO NOAH WITH MAIL
WATER BILL
MPIE

AND NOAH RELEASED THE ANIMALS FROM THE ARK.
MPE

NOAH'S
FLOOD
REUNION
WAIT. WAIT. DON'T TELL ME. B-LEVEL, SECTION 23, STALL 5... RIGHT?
BEAR
MPIE

GOOD OL'
BOYS

CIRCUMCISION WASN'T AN EASY THING FOR ABRAHAM TO EXPLAIN TO HIS HOUSEHOLD.

LOT'S FAMILY PORTRAIT

MPIÉ

AND LOT WAS LAID TO REST
HERE LIES LOT
SODIUM FREE
MPIE

THIS WASN'T a GOOD TIME FOR ISaaC TO BRING UP THE aLLOWaNCE ISSUE
MDE

OLD Isaac CONFUSED a LOT OF THINGS WITH Esau.
HELLO, My SON.
MPE

JACOB VS ANGEL:
THE RE-MATCH IS ON.
COMING
JULY 9TH
TO THE HEBREW ARENA

JOSEPH WAS SOLD TO ISHMAELITES TRAVELING TO EGYPT IN A CARAVAN
EGYPT
457A1
MPE

POOR JOB. AS IF THINGS WEREN'T BAD ENOUGH.

PATRIARCH COMMERCIAL
IF YOU'VE EVER SUFFERED FROM PAIN & ITCH OF BOILS, TRY
JOB'S POTSHERDS.
THEY SCRATCH WHERE IT ITCHES OR YOUR MONEY BACK
J

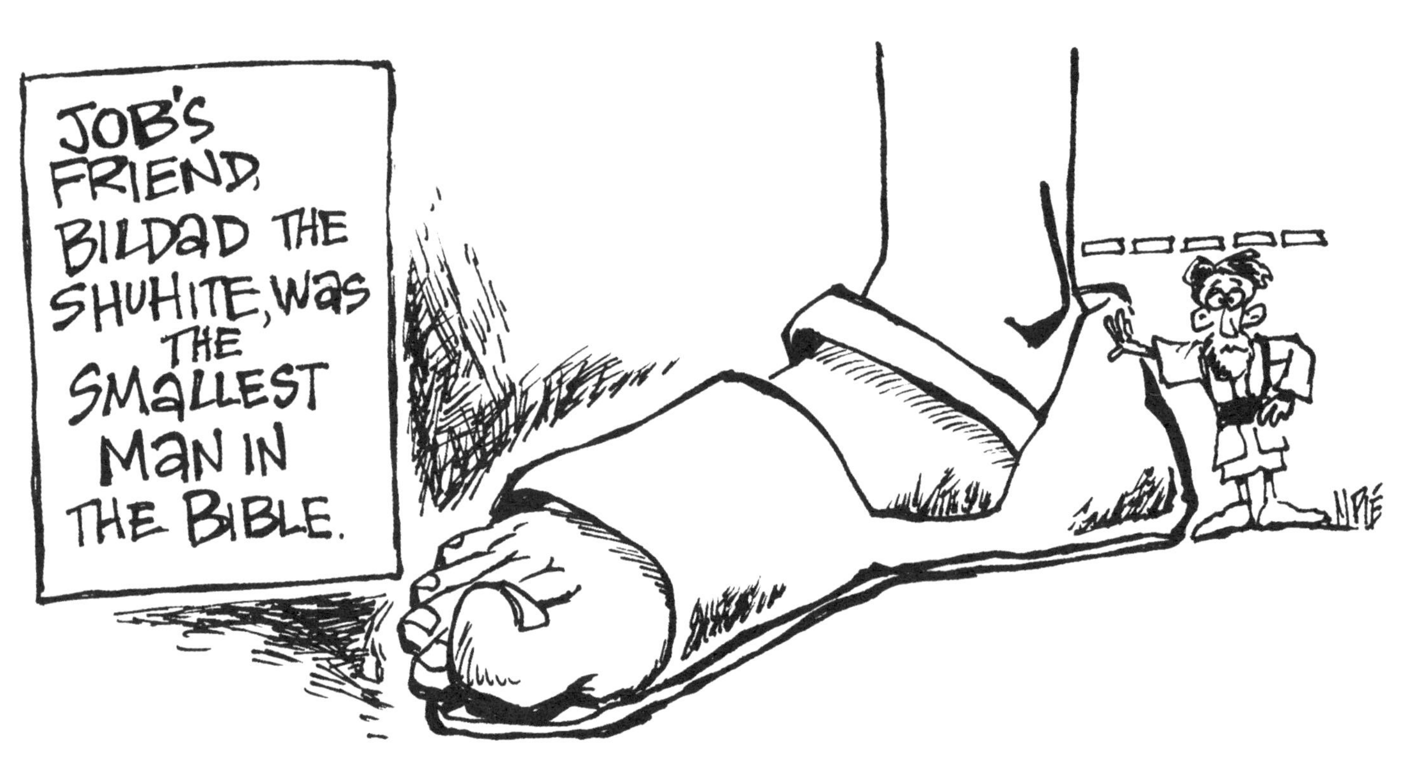
JOB'S FRIEND, BILDAD THE SHUHITE, WAS THE SMALLEST MAN IN THE BIBLE.
NPIE

FINALLY JOB HAD SOME GOOD NEWS. HE JUST SAVED A BUNCH OF MONEY ON HIS CAR INSURANCE.
SAUF

MOSES
Ho Ho's

MOSES' RECURRING NIGHTMARE

AARON NEVER KNEW WHEN MOSES' ROD WOULD SUDDENLY START ACTING UP.
MPLÉ

MOSES MEETS an EXPERT ON RODS THAT TURN INTO SNAKES
CRIKEY! BE CAREFUL, MATE.
a BITE FROM THIS GIRL IS REALLY PaINFUL

NOW WE TURN TO NILE 5 WEaTHER.
THERE IS a DENSE FROG ADVISORY IN EFFECT FOR YOUR MORNING COMMUTE.

ANOTHER
EGYPTIAN PLAGUE:
FREQUENT
CABLE OUTAGES.
AAUH!

ANOTHER UNRECORDED EGYPTIAN PLAGUE:
BABYLONIAN TELEMARKETERS
CONGRATULATIONS!
BLAW! BLAW! BLAW! BLAW!
MPIE

MURPHY'S LAW WAS WRITTEN BY MURPHY, THE EGYPTIAN, AFTER WHAT "COULD" GO WRONG... "DID"!

THINGS THAT WOULD HAVE BEEN GOOD TO HAVE AT THE MOMENT
EGYPTIAN SUBMARINES AT THE RED SEA
EGYPT 1

NOBODY TOLD OMAR THE CATFISH THAT THE RED SEA WAS PARTED.

RED Sea FISH STORY
I'M SERIOUS! THERE WERE MILLIONS OF HUMANS WALKIN' RIGHT PAST ME!!!
FELLas!
MPiE

a COMMON PROBLEM WITH LIVING IN THE WILDERNESS WERE THOSE EMBARRASSING UPDRAFTS
SIGH
MPIÉ

WHAT IF IT
WAS PIZZA
INSTEAD OF
MANNA?
DANG! I HATE MUSHROOMS.
I WANTED EXTRA CHEESE.

MOSES WONDERED WHAT THIS STRANGE SIGN IN THE SKY COULD MEAN.

MOSES SAW ANOTHER STRANGE SIGN IN THE WILDERNESS SKY.
CONSTRUCTION AHEAD NEXT 5000 MILES

INDIANA SON OF JONES... ARE YOU SURE YOU ARE A LEVITE?

ANOTHER STRANGE SIGN IN THE WILDERNESS SKY
TUNNEL AHEAD. REMOVE YOUR SUNGLASSES
DMRE

THE HEBREWS
SENT SPIES
INTO THE
LAND OF
JERICHO

RAHAB SHOULD HAVE USED A LONGER ROPE TO HELP THE SPIES ESCAPE
AAAH!!
MPIE

THE JERICHO INSURANCE COMPANY WAS VERY BUSY THAT NEXT DAY.
HELLO? NO! NOT COVERED! ...ACT OF GOD!
MPE

MOSES
MEETS
CHARLTON
HESTON

GIANT
"GAGS"

GOLIATH DIDN'T HAVE THE TEMPERAMENT FOR THE SECRETARY JOB
WELCOME
MPIE

GOLIATH as a STATE TROOPER
SAYS HERE YOUR NAME IS DAVID?
MPIE

CAN YOU IMAGINE GOLIATH WITH A SENSITIVE SIDE?
MPE

GOLIATH
HAD A
VERY
EASY
STRIKE
ZONE

WHAT IF DAVID'S SHOT WASN'T HARD ENOUGH?
OW... GEEZ! WHY YOU LITTLE...

THE PHILISTINE
COACH IS
CHALLENGING
THE RULING
ON THE
FIELD.

GOLIATH'S HEAD WAS SOLD AS A HOME SECURITY DEVICE
HEY!
MDÉ

GOLIATH HAD BROTHERS. AND EVERY ONE OF THEM SENT DAVID A BIRTHDAY CARD.
GOLIATH'S BROTHER
DAVID

HERE COME
THE JUDGES

SOME OF GIDEON'S MEN DRANK WATER LIKE A DOG. BUT THEIR DOGS DRANK LIKE MEN.
MDIE

YES.
I PAID
MY LIFE
INSURANCE
PREMIUM.
WHY?

THINGS THAT WOULD HAVE BEEN GOOD TO HAVE AT THE MOMENT

YOUNG DAVID'S TEENAGE VOICE-CRACKING PROBLEM BOTHERED HIS SHEEP
MPÉ

THINGS THAT WOULD HAVE BEEN GOOD TO HAVE AT THE MOMENT

a KING DAVID TEMPTATION BUSTER

ABSOLOM
was also
CREDITED
FOR
INVENTING
THE FIRST
SUN DIAL

as a Baby,
HE Was ONE
OF SOLOMON'S
FaIRNESS LESSONS
GONE BaD.
MRE

EVEN WISE KING SOLOMON HAD TROUBLE SOLVING MATHEMATICAL WORD PROBLEMS.
NOAH'S 2 CAMELS EACH DRINK 19.6 GALS. OF WATER PER DAY. HOW MANY GALLONS SHOULD NOAH BRING ON THE ARK PER CAMEL FOR A YEAR LONG TRIP?

NO ONE COULD EVER BEAT SOLOMON AT JEOPARDY
I'LL TAKE "WISDOM FOR 1000," ALEX.
100.000

PROPHETS
& LAFFS

Balaam's Donkey DIDN'T STOP at "TalKING..."
My KIND OF TOWN, JERUSalEM IS...
MPIE

ELIJAH MAKING SURE THAT GOD'S AIM WAS GOOD
FIRE
MPLE

ELIJAH AND
HIS FIERY
CHARIOT
ARRIVE IN
HEAVEN.
MPIE

DANIEL'S CONFIDENCE GREW WITH EVERY PASSING MINUTE
MPE

WHAT IF DANIEL WAS CAST INTO A DEN OF HUNGRY CUB SCOUTS

WHAT IF THE HAND WRITING ON THE WALL WAS MISSPELLED
YOU HAVE BEEN W IN THE BALANCE
MPIÉ

JONAH THOUGHT HE WAS ALONE IN THE WHALE'S BELLY.

THINGS THAT WOULD HAVE BEEN GOOD TO HAVE AT THE MOMENT

WHALE
WHALE REPELLANT
(UNFORTUNATELY FOR JONAH)
ONLY AVAILABLE IN NINEVAH

FISH BIBLE STORIES
AND THEN, JONAH THE FISH-PROPHET, WAS SWALLOWED UP BY A GREAT HUMAN.
MPLF

IT'S Easy
TO SPOT
a PROPHET
at THE BEACH

DISCIPLINE WAS ENFORCED AT THE SCHOOL OF THE PROPHETS
I will not prop
I will not prophesy falsely
I will not prophesy falsely
prophesy falsely
prophesy falsely
prophesy falsely
prophesy falsely
prophesy falsely
prophesy falsely
prophesy falsely
prophesy falsely
I will not prophesy falsely
I will not prophesy falsely
MPIE

MAJOR PROPHET.
MINOR PROPHET.
SUBSTANTIAL LOSS.
ISAIAH
JOEL
HOMELESS

WHY SOME MINOR PROPHETS NEVER BECAME MAJOR PROPHETS_
WELCOME PROPHET CONVENTION
MDIE

THINGS YOU CAN MAKE WITH A FALSE PROPHET
A DOOR STOP
OOFF!
MPIE

a GOOD PUNISHMENT FOR a FalSE PROPHET
DEMONSTRATION MODEL FOR a Hair REMOVaL PRODUCT.
R-R-RIP!
MPIE

THINGS YOU CAN MAKE WITH A FALSE PROPHET
A PIÑATA FOR A GORILLA PARTY

a GOOD PUNISHMENT FOR a FalSE PROPHET
JUDGE a BLACKBOaRD-SCRaTCHING CONTEST
SCREEK!
CONTESTANT #6
JUDGE
LUPIE

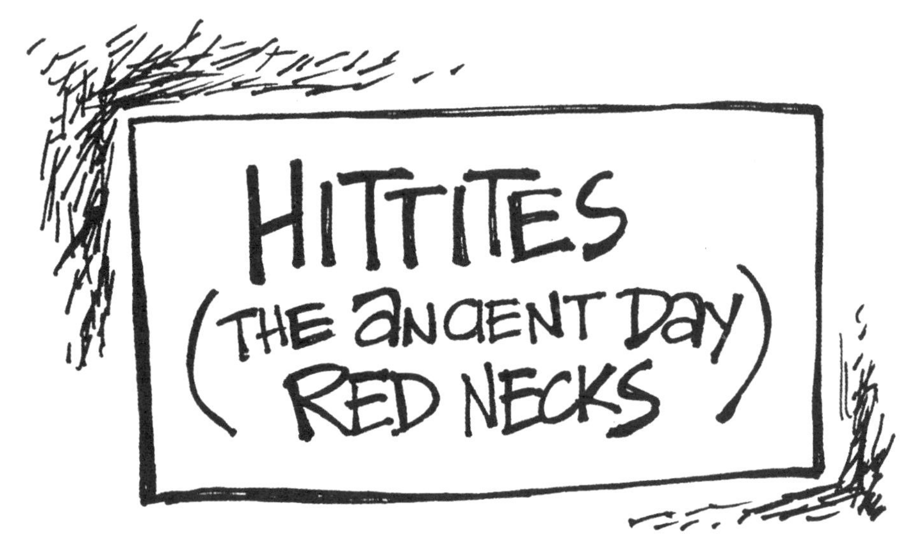
HITTITES
(THE ancient Day
RED NECKS)

YOU KNOW YOU'RE A HITTITE WHEN...
YOU HAVE MORE THAN 2 CHARIOTS UP ON BLOCKS IN YOUR YARD.
MPIE

YOU KNOW YOU'RE A HITTITE WHEN...
YOUR BELTBUCKLE IS ALMOST AS BIG AS YOUR SHIELD

YOU KNOW YOU'RE a HITTITE WOMAN WHEN...
YOUR BEHIVE HaIR DO IS FUNCTIONAL
MPIÉ

YOU KNOW YOU'RE a HITTITE WHEN...
YOU WORSHIP THE GOD "MULLET".
MULLET

YOU KNOW YOU'RE A HITTITE WHEN...
"NAME THAT ROAD KILL" IS A POPULAR FAMILY TRAVELING GAME.
SQUIRREL!

YOU KNOW YOU'RE A HITTITE WHEN...
all YOUR CALENDARS HAVE RACEY LOOKING HORSES ON THEM.
SPEED
POWER
1 2 3 4 5 6 7
8 9 10 11 12 13 14
JANUARY
1 2 3 4 5 6 7
8 9 10 11 12 13 14
15 16 17 18 19 20 21

"NT"
HUMOR

AND MARY SPAKE UNTO THE SHEPHERDS SAYING...
WASH YOUR HANDS!

THE SAVIOR'S FIRST
VIEW OF HIS PEOPLE

THE 3 WISE MEN DIDN'T FEEL SO WISE WHEN THEY SAW THE 24% INTEREST RATE ON THEIR CREDIT CARD BILL.

THERE WAS GOLD, FRANKINCENSE AND MYRRH. BUT WHO GAVE THE FRUIT CAKE?
MPIE

BIBLICAL DILEMMA:
HOW SHOULD CARPENTER
JOSEPH RESPOND WHEN
HIS SAVIOR-SON IS
STANDING WITHIN
EARSHOT?

NT2

THEY CALL HIM JOHN THE SOUTHERN BAPTIST

JOHN THE BAPTIST DOING SOME GROCERY SHOPPING

JOHN THE BAPTIST SNACK FOOD
HOT
SPICEY LOCUSTS
HONEY GLAZED BUGS
NPB

IF YOU "DO" HIDE YOUR LIGHT UNDER a BASKET,
BE CAREFUL
MPLÉ

EVEN THE **THOUGHT** OF HAVING A "LOG IN YOUR OWN EYE" IS PAINFUL.
MPIE

THINGS THAT WOULD HAVE BEEN GOOD TO HAVE AT THE MOMENT
DEMON EJECTION BUTTON
MPIE

THERE'S always a WISE GUY IN THE BUNCH
MPE

...AND LAZARUS WAS UNWRAPPED!

THE VERY HAIRS OF YOUR HEAD ARE NUMBERED.
57
58
59
60
61
62
63
65
66
213
214
215
216
217
218
230
231
232
233

HAVE YOU SEEN THAT CROWD? IT'S GONNA TAKE A MIRACLE TO STRETCH US THAT FAR.
MPE

PETER'S FAITH TO WALK ON WATER WAS CLEARLY SHAKEN

INSENSITIVE THINGS TO SAY TO PETER:
WILL YOU WALK OUT ON THE WATER AND GET MY HAT?
NATE

JAMES MISUNDERSTOOD THE MASTER'S COMMAND TO "TELL THE VISION" TO NO ONE.
NRE

JUST BEFORE THE MIRACLE...
PARDON ME. IS THERE A... "COIN" IN MY MOUTH?
MPIE

AND THEY FOUND THE COLT TIED JUST AS THE MASTER SAID.
75
75
NPLÉ

HE SAID HE WAS "IN" THE FIG TREE WHEN IT WAS CURSED.
MPIÉ

THINGS THAT WOULD HAVE BEEN GOOD TO HAVE AT THE MOMENT
THE PHARISEE BOOK OF PITHY COME-BACKS
MPIE

ANOTHER INSENSITIVE THING TO SAY TO PETER:
ANYBODY WANT TO PLAY "PIN-THE-EAR-ON THE-SERVANT-OF THE-HIGH-PRIEST"?
MCPHEE

SCRIPTURE SAYS, THERE WAS NO SMALL DISPUTATION BETWEEN PAUL AND BARNABAS

PAUL WAS GREETED BY THE NATIVES ON THE ISLAND WHERE HE WAS SHIPWRECKED.

PETER'S FIRST UNSUCCESSFUL attempt TO FISH FOR MEN
MPÉ

PHARISEES
NEED NOT
APPLY

NOT a GOOD JOB FOR an UNEMPLOYED PHARISEE
Day Care WORKER
MPIÉ

NOT a GOOD JOB FOR an UNEMPLOYED PHARISEE
RODEO CLOWN

NOT a GOOD JOB FOR an UNEMPLOYED PHARISEE.
RUNWAY MODEL

NOT a GOOD JOB FOR an UNEMPLOYED PHARISEE
Rap artist
MPE

NOT a GOOD JOB FOR an UNEMPLOYED PHaRISEE
OLYMPIC SWIMMER
1
2
3

ETCETERa
ETCETERa
ETCETERa

IF "ANGELS BOWLING" MAKES THUNDER, THIS WAS A GUTTER BALL
BONK!
MPE

DON'T YOU JUST LOVE THAT NEW CAMEL SMELL?
HABEEB'S CAMELS
SALE
MPIE

CLOUD CHAIRS IN HEAVEN ARE HARD TO GET USED TO
UPIÉ

YOU KNOW, THEY always KILL THE "FaTTED" CALF.
MATÉ

YES! GOD DOES HAVE a BIG DOG.
MPIE

HELL HAS NO HOLIDAYS

WELL... OK! "ONE" HOLIDAY.

AND SOME SEED FELL IN JACK'S GARDEN.

THE ROMAN
UMPIRE

THE JEWS LOOKED FOR SIGNS
ONE WAY
STOP
EXIT
YIELD
NO PARKING THIS SIDE
OH THESE ARE NICE.

THIS IS ONE TRIO THAT DEFINITELY WOULD NOT MAKE IT THROUGH THE FIERY FURNACE
I CAN'T SEE. I CAN'T SEE. I GOT MY EYES CLOSED.
SPREAD OUT!
WOOH WOOH WOOH
MPIE

THE GOOD,
THE BAD
AND THE FUNNY

GOOD IDEA

HUMBLE YOURSELF.

HUMILIATE YOURSELF.

GOOD IDEA

BY FAITH, MOVE MOUNTAINS AND CAST THEM INTO THE SEA.

BAD IDEA

NOT GETTING OFF THE MOUNTAIN FIRST.

AAAH

GOOD IDEA

BEING TRANSPORTED AFTER YOU BAPTIZE SOMEONE.

BAD IDEA

BEING TRANSPORTED TO A ROMAN GUARD HOUSE.

GOOD IDEA:
BUILD YOUR HOUSE
ON A ROCK

BAD IDEA:
BUILD YOUR HOUSE
UNDER A ROCK

Photo: Patti Brahim

About the Author...

Mark Pié is a professional cartoonist currently living in Pittsburgh, PA. He and his wife Karen have been married for 30 years and have been blessed with great kids, all of whom are walking with the Lord. Mark received his graphic arts training at the Art Institute of Pittsburgh where he majored in Cartooning and Animation. After graduating in 1973, he spent most of his professional career in the graphic arts industry, with his most memorable opportunity serving as the Art Director of ***New Wine Magazine*** (a Christian, non-denominational magazine) in the 70's and the 80's. It was there his cartoon skills began to take shape. Mark has been keeping people laughing ever since!

Mark Pié is available for humorous talks and presentations.
For more information write:

Mark Pié
433 Highland Road
Pittsburgh, PA 15235